Tarantula Spiders

by Claire Archer

capstone

Tarantula Spiders © 2016 by ABDO. All Rights Reserved. This version distributed and published by Capstone Classroom © 2016 with the permission of ABDO.

International copyrights reserved in all countries. No part of this book may be reproduced in any form without written permission from the publisher.

Photo Credits: Shutterstock, Thinkstock

Production Contributors: Teddy Borth, Jennie Forsberg, Grace Hansen

Design Contributors: Dorothy Toth, Laura Rask

Library of Congress Cataloging-in-Publication data is available on the Library of Congress Website.

ISBN 978-1-4966-0980-9 (paperback)

Printed and bound in the USA.
009942F16

Table of Contents

Tarantulas 4

Food 14

Baby Tarantulas 20

More Facts 22

Glossary 23

Index 24

Tarantulas

Tarantulas can be found in many places around the world. They mainly live in dry deserts and grasslands.

Some tarantulas live in burrows.
Others live in trees or under
rocks and leaves.

7

Most tarantulas are black or brown. Some can be very colorful.

Tarantulas are hairy spiders. Even their eight legs are covered with hair.

10

Tarantulas come in all sizes. Some are tiny. Some can be as big as a dinner plate!

Food

When hunting, a tarantula will hide and wait for its **prey**.

Then it pounces on its prey.

The tarantula bites its prey. Then it injects venom that paralyzes its prey.

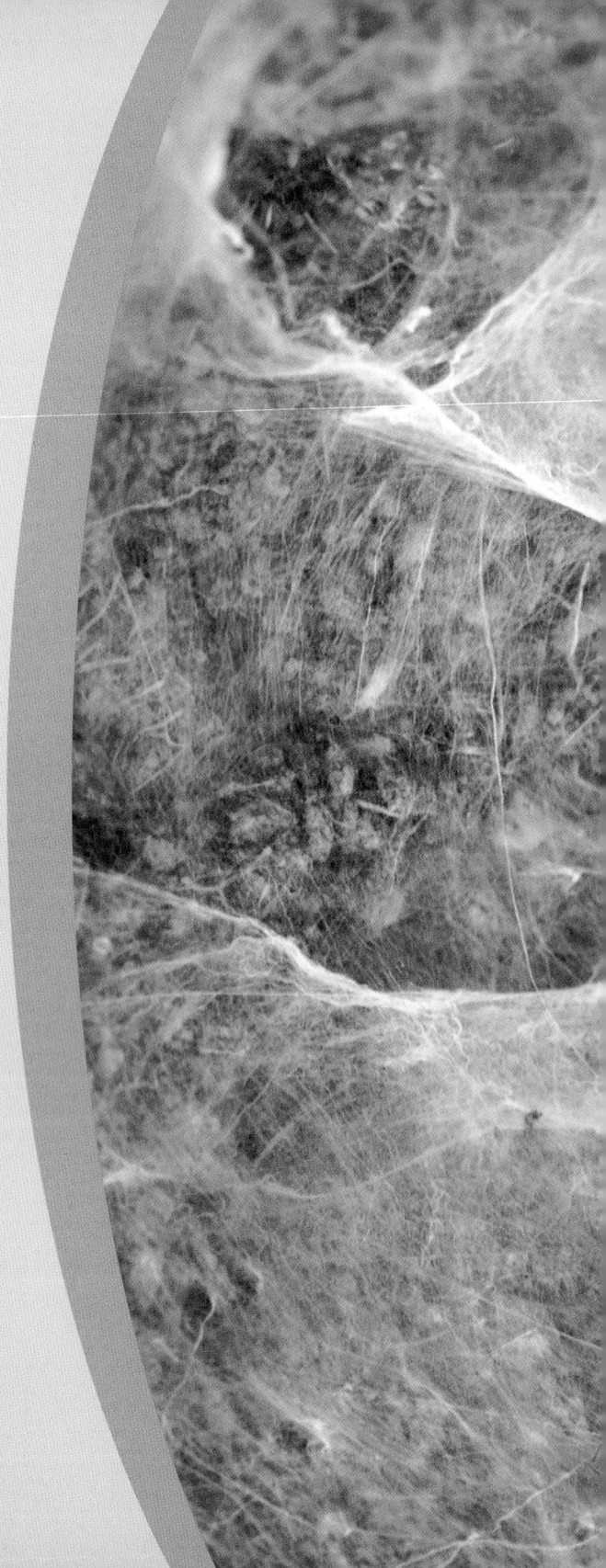

Tarantulas eat many animals. They like insects and other spiders. They like mice and birds too.

19

Baby Tarantulas

Female tarantulas lay several hundred eggs at a time. When they hatch, the baby spiders are called **spiderlings**.

More Facts

- Tarantulas that live in burrows dig them with their fangs. Some steal other tarantulas' homes!

- The tarantula's worst predator is the spider-wasp.

- Some people have pet tarantulas!

Glossary

burrow - an animal's underground home.

paralyze - to cause a loss of motion or feeling in a part of the body.

prey - an animal hunted or killed by a predator for food.

spiderling – a baby spider.

venom - a poison made by some animals and insects. It usually enters a victim through a bite or a sting.

Index

baby tarantulas 20
burrow 6
color 8
desert 4
eggs 20
food 18
grassland 4
habitat 4
hair 10
hunting 14
legs 10
prey 14, 16
size 12
venom 16